Self-Love (Now)

Mahogany Clark
Self-Published
Quote Book

Copyright© 2024 Mahogany Clark

All rights reserved. Without limiting the rights under

copyright reserved above. No part of this book may be.

reproduced into any sort of retrieval system, or

transmitted into any form, or by any means (electronic,

mechanical, photocopying, recording, or otherwise)

without the prior written consent from the author, except

brief quotes used in reviews, interviews, or magazines.

Table of contents

The Ugly... 1
The Bad..34
The Good..64

The ugly

"If you could talk to your 19-year-old self, what would you say? I would tell her, you are loveable, you are worthy, and you are more powerful than you know. You are and have everything money cannot buy and that is what makes you more than worth it." - Mahoganywritez

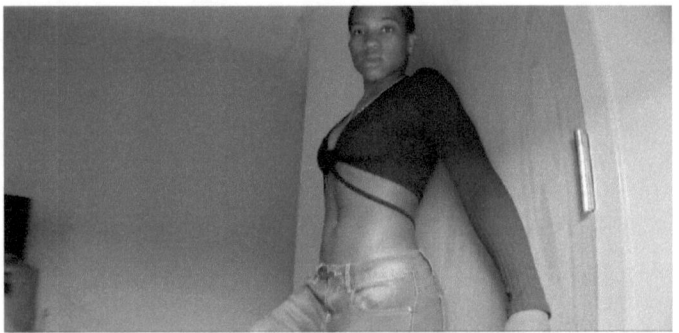

The ugly

"Rushing thoughts, going through my head, the only time I catch a break is when I am sleeping or when I am dead." - Mahoganywritez

The ugly

"My anxiety is my worst enemy, from the moments I open my eyes, I can't stop these thoughts from crowding me." —Mahoganywritez

The ugly

"I have had to go through all my toughest, and some of my best moments alone, and when I fall, I have no one to lean on." - Mahoganywritez

The ugly

"Suicidal thoughts have run through my head, sometimes I would think I am just better off dead, why am I here what purpose do I serve. Why did I deserve to be born into so much hurt?" —Mahoganywritez

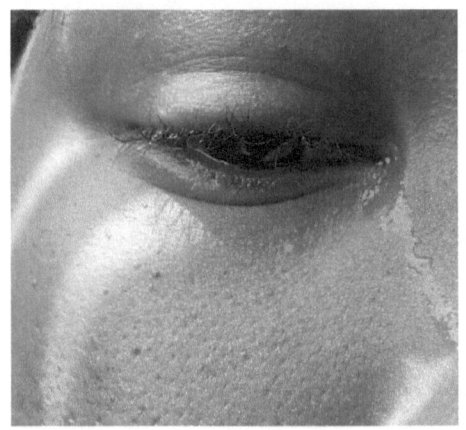

The ugly

"I have loved people more than I love myself, if they are happy, I do not need anything else." —Mahoganywritez

The ugly

"Why am I not enough, why can't I have what I want, to be happy and at peace, with someone that loves me, is too much for me to ask for." —Mahoganywritez

The Ugly

"Why was I born? I have asked myself this time & time in life at each stage, child, teenage, and even adult. A person with no purpose is like a crab with no shell." — Mahoganywritez

The ugly

"When you feel numb to everything, and any emotion it is like floating. No substance, just a heartbeat, feeling emptiness is too close to being dead." —Mahoganywritez

The ugly

"Empty is what many of us feel or felt. So, we distract ourselves from the feeling, with drugs, parties, sex, or even our friends. You could be talking to someone and have no idea how empty they feel." —Mahoganywritez

The ugly

"Hearing your parents tell you I don't want you is one of the coldest things you could hear, and in adult hood when you feel unwanted it is more than likely a result of those moments." -Mahoganywritez

The ugly

"All I did was walk in the room, and I did not even say anything. However, people are so ready to make sure I know they are better than me. If only they knew the inside struggles, I fight through mentally." - Mahoganywritez

The ugly

"Strong Independent Black woman, something I never called myself, but people label me before I can even speak." —Mahoganywritez

The ugly

"It is just funny how when you are as genuine as you can be, people still find a reason to discredit me." —Mahoganywritez

The ugly

The	Sky	But
Touch		All
Can		In
You		The
Like		Same
Feel		Moment
You		You
High		Can
So		Feel
Be		So
Can		Low.
You
∧
Mahoganywritez

The ugly

"I don't know what I am destined to be but sometimes this life be killing me, and my thoughts are a burden that weigh so heavily on me." —Mahoganywritez

The ugly

"If your home is not where you can find peace is it even home at all?" —Mahoganywritez

The Ugly

"I guess because someone puts clothes on your back and a roof over your head it gives them the right to abuse you, whenever they get the chance, but I almost would rather be poor and homeless instead". -Mahoganywritez

The ugly

"I just want to be free, but my thoughts keep trapping me, I want my peace of mind and my sense of sanity." —Mahoganywritez

The ugly

"Self-esteem issues, will you have you around the wrong people, giving to the wrong people, and begging people to stay." —Mahoganywritez

The ugly

"You know how they say music soothes the savage beast, well that & my pen and paper are what soothes me" —Mahoganywritez

The ugly

"Heavy hearts, weigh a lot, it just feels like you're carrying the world on your shoulders but in your heart." —Mahoganywritez

The ugly

"My pain is like a migraine that won't go away" -Mahoganywritez

The Ugly

"Words can cut really deep; I would know because I still carry some words that was uttered to me when I was a child" - Mahoganywritez

The ugly

"My cries seem to go unheard, and my pain unfelt, I don't know how much longer I have in me left" - Mahoganywritez

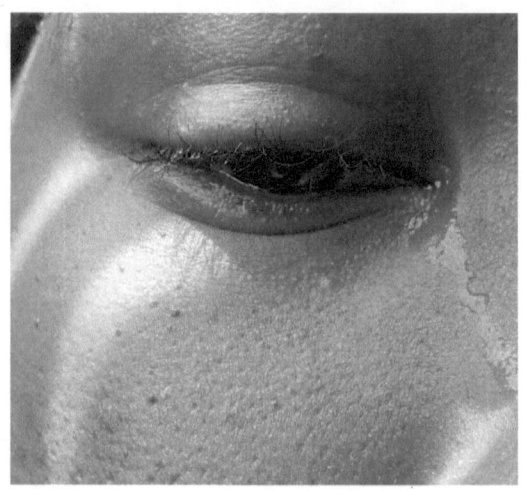

The ugly

"I want to be free, from these shackles and chains, my heart hurts and my body aches" - Mahoganywritez

The ugly

"Everything hits harder than before, and the pain seems to linger longer" -Mahoganywritez

The ugly

"Give me my peace, you can keep everything else, give me my peace because I don't want to bleed insanity" —Mahoganywritez

The Ugly

"We spend too much time trying to fill that void that burns inside, with everyone, and everything but what we really need" - Mahoganywritez

The ugly

"When asked would you rather have respect or love, I used to say love, because that's how much I was missing it" - Mahoganywritrez

The Bad

"Therapy, won't change anything I used to say, but then I was hurting so much I was willing to try anything"- Mahoganywritez

The Bad

"I'm talking but there is only so much that talking does for me." —Mahoganywritez

The Bad

"If I had to say my creative moments are the only thing that made me happy and saved me."
—Mahoganywritez

The Bad

"Overthinking can either be my worst enemy or my best friend." —Mahoganywritez

The Bad

"Sometimes I can hardly stop my thoughts from happening, it's like they control me" - Mahoganywritez

The Bad

"Catastrophizing, has become a part of me, I instantly proceed to the worst possible outcome, of any situation" —Mahoganywritez

The Bad

"I don't have to many people around, because I see things on a deeper level that they don't" —Mahoganywritez

The Bad

"isn't it funny when you try to avoid people to avoid being used or hurt and still be taken advantage of by those closest to you" - Mahoganywritez

The Bad

"I find it hard to say no, because I don't want to make them feel bad, just shows my lack of self-boundaries" -Mahoganywritez

The Bad

"You know you love someone as much as you say you do based off how much you're willing to sacrifice for them" —Mahoganywritez

The Bad

"My abandonment wounds run deep, and I feel down when people ignore or leave me." - Mahoganywritez

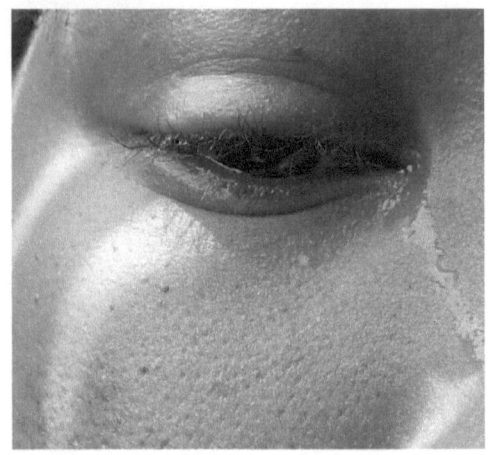

The Bad

"I was feeling pain so long in life, I just expected to always feel it moving forward" - Mahoganywritez

The Bad

"I would rather end a connection before it leaves my life, because eventually it doesn't last." —Mahoganywritez

The Bad

"Sometimes, I just feel like FML" - Mahoganywritez

The Bad

"All my creations started with me feeling pain, but my creations are also the reason I want to live" —Mahoganywritez

The Bad

"Even though, the world doesn't care about your pain I have never been afraid to share mine" -Mahoganywritez

The Bad

"I just wanted someone to care about me as much, I cared for people" -Mahoganywritez

The Bad

"I feel too strongly about things, that's why I can only have a few people around" - Mahoganywritez

The Bad

"I'm too emotional, or people just don't care as much as they used to" -Mahoganywritez

The Bad

"I'm just searching for a reason to live" - Mahoganywritez

The Bad

"I have a great memory, and I can recall my painful memories vividly" —Mahoganywritez

The Bad

"They say nothing last forever, but something has to at least last a lifetime" - Mahoganywritez

The Bad

"I could show someone that I loved them in a million ways, but could barely show myself love"
—Mahoganywritez

The Bad

"Low self-esteem really has you doing somethings that you will regret" - Mahoganywritez

The Bad

"You ever just think to yourself what's wrong with me, what am I missing" —Mahoganywritez

The Bad

"I tried to get away from my trauma to only go through more, I guess you can't shortcut the process" —Mahoganywritez

The Bad

"It's amazing how other people can see how great you before you" —Mahoganywritez

The Bad

"I used to find happiness, fulfilment and even a sense of self in pleasing others" - Mahoganywritez

The Bad

"Some moments you're up and some you're down, sometimes you wonder why you had to have so many downs to finally get up and stay there" —Mahoganywritez

The Bad

"The truth about any healing journey is there are plenty of ugly moments and restarts" - Mahoganywritez

The Good

"I had to learn how to be alone and get away from being lonely" -Mahoganywritez

The Good

"it's ok to burn some bridges and let go of things no longer serving you" —Mahoganywritez

The Good

"One of the hardest things to do is to take self-accountability for the things you allowed"
—Mahoganywritez

The Good

"Emotional management will give you so much peace and save you so much stress" - Mahoganywritez

The Good

"I have and will do the deep work on myself that people never take out the time to do" - Mahoganywritez

The Good

"It's ok to forgive yourself and move forward"
-Mahoganywritez

The Good

"You can have the knowledge but without the experience it's still unfamiliar and unrelatable"
—Mahoganywritez

The Good

"You know you love someone as much as you say do based on how much you are willing to sacrifice, but be careful sacrificing you" - Mahoganywritez

The Good

"You must fall in love with every version of you, and embrace yourself" —Mahoganywritez

The Good

"Everything you are looking for on the outside you have it in you the entire time" - Mahoganywritez

The Good

"Sometimes people can see who you are before you even know who you are" -Mahoganywritez

The Good

"No one will care and love you like you, love and care for yourself" —Mahoganywritez

The Good

"It's ok to be selfish, sometimes, because if you are not good then everything around you won't thrive either" -Mahoganywritez

The Good

"You have to stand on your word not only to those around you but the word to yourself" - Mahoganywritez

The Good

"You owe yourself" —Mahoganywritez

The Good

"Everyone is not meant to have a piece of you" —Mahoganywritez

The Good

"Feel what you have to feel, cry about it, but you have to get up" —Mahoganywritez

The Good

"The power to give is beautiful, so don't miss out on giving to yourself" -Mahoganywritez

The Good

"You are imperfectly perfect" -Mahoganywritez

The Good

"How much are you worth to you?" - Mahoganywritez

The Good

"When you start to do better for yourself somethings will fall apart" -Mahoganywritez

The Good

"Sometimes your expectations for people will cause you the most pains" -Mahoganywritez

The Good

"I learned to expect people to do what is best for themselves" -Mahoganywritez

The Good

"Keeping a light heart after the pain is what free looks like" -Mahoganywritez

The Good

"Acceptance will help you in every stage of life" —Mahoganywritez

The Good

"Real love doesn't hurt" -Mahoganywritez

The Good

"Make sure that you are ok" —Mahoganywritez

The Good

"Think of ways to improve yourself everyday" - Mahoganywritez

The Good

"Find things that you like about yourself, and what you like to do" —Mahoganywritez

The Good

"It is ok to be vulnerable" —Mahoganywritez

The Good

"Everyone has intuition use it" -
Mahoganywritez

The Good

"The reason we feel entitled is to overcompensate from past maltreatment" - Mahoganywritez

The Good

"Once your eyes have been opened there is no closing them back" -Mahoganywritez

The Good

"If you have been persevering and you began to feel like giving up that means you are close to your triumph" —Mahoganywritez

The Good

"The inside is more important than the outside, but they are both important" —Mahoganywritez

The Good

"The self-love journey is not just about loving yourself; it is also about the moments that you did not" —Mahoganywritez

The Good

"Be kind to yourself" —Mahoganywritez

The Good

"Every journey is different but relatable in the same way" —Mahoganywritez

The Good

"I am Mahogany, and I am everything that money can't buy" —Mahoganywritez

The Good

"Self-Love is the best love" —Mahoganywritez

Email:Borntosoar81@gmail.com

Instagram: @Mahoganywritez

Facebook: Mahogany Clark/Mahoganywritez

www.ingramcontent.com/pod-product-compliance
Lightning Source LLC
LaVergne TN
LVHW041711060526
838201LV00043B/686